Praise for *Letting Go*

I0151894

Letting Go is a heartfelt book. Within it, pain and tenderness are equally acknowledged, one often intensifying the other. Parents, spouses, children, and flowers all blossom on the page, nurtured by a mature imagination and the courage of clarity. Both newcomers to contemporary poetry and experienced readers will find much to treasure here.

Gilbert Allen
author of *Driving to Distraction* (2003) and
Second Chances (1991)
winner of the 2007 Robert Penn Warren Prize in Poetry from
The Southern Review

Reading the poems of Donna Lisle Burton is like happening upon a cache of tender and beautifully crafted love letters. Among the objects of her most intimate affections are lovers both old and new — parents and siblings and children; students and friends; flowers and bridges and mills. And, finally, her luckiest of lovers, whoever might open the pages of this exquisite book."

Cathy Smith Bowers
author of *Like Shining from Shook Foil* (2010) and
A Book of Minutes (2004)
Poet Laureate of NC 2010-2012,
winner of the Gilbert-Chappell
Distinguished Poet Award (2006, 2007)

With grace and skill, Donna Burton reminds us of our connections to each other and the places we inhabit. Love, in all its myriad manifestations, permeates these poems. Whether addressing the long-lost young love of her parents, love for her students, love lost or unspeakable acts, Burton embraces all with compassion, finding in each that "single breath of beauty."

Do not be misled by the title: once you start reading, there will be no Letting Go. "Let something, then, claim you / that you cannot shake loose," Burton writes in one poem. These poems do just that, so come, let them claim you.

Pat Riviere-Seel
author of *No Turning Back Now* (2004)
winner of the 2009 Roanoke-Chowan Award for Poetry from the
NC Literary and Historical Society for *The Serial Killer's Daughter* (2009)

LETTING GO

Donna Lisle Burton

POEMS
1983-2003

P

Pisgah Press

Pisgah Press was established in 2011 to publish and promote works of quality offering original ideas and insight into the human condition, the realm of knowledge, and the world around us.

Printed in the United States of America

Published by Pisgah Press, LLC
PO Box 1427, Candler, NC 28715
www.pisgahpress.com

Cover photography by Donna Lisle Burton
Cover design & layout by A. D. Reed

All photographs and art reproduced in this book
are by Donna Lisle Burton

Library of Congress Cataloging-in-Publication Data
Burton, Donna Lisle
Letting Go: Poems 1983-2003
Donna Lisle Burton

Library of Congress Control Number: 2012935775

ISBN: 978-0985387501
Poetry/General

Originally printed in 2003 by Indexx, Inc., Greenville, SC

First Pisgah Press Edition
Third Printing
July 2014

For my first loves,
Cassia and Tim,
and my newest loves,
grandson, Dean, and
husband, Alan

Thanks to Gilbert Allen and Cathy Smith Bowers for seeing my passion and helping me to harness it.

"Nobody can tell me what to write because nobody pulls my strings. I have not been writing to make money or earn my living. I have taught school as my vocation. Writing is my life but it is an avocation nobody can buy."

Margaret Walker
"The Writer on Her Work"
p. 101

Acknowledgements

The author wishes to thank the editors of the following publications where these words first appeared:

Atlanta Review	"Pneumonia"
The Aurorean	"South Carolina Spring"
Earthbound	"To You, Old Lover, Wherever You Are"
	"Mark the Epileptic"
	"To My Sixteen Year Old Whom I Do Not Love Enough"
	"Upon My Nine-Year-Old's Return from Summer Camp"
	"Dilettante"
	"Song on Hallowed Eve"
	"City Fall"
The Iconoclast	"Old Lady Teaching in Locker Room"
Illuminations	"Doing It Over"
	"Decision"
Kalliope	"Birdie"
Licking River Review	"Thirteen-Inch Snowfall in Tuskegee, Alabama"
Main Street Rag	"The Mills"
	"Leaving"
Minnesota Review	"Impetuosity"
Owen Wister Review	"Words Retrieved"
Plainsongs	"Falling in Love With the Boy from across the Ohio River"
Potpourri	"To a Friend, Lately Divorced and Childless"
Southern Poetry Review	"The Untouchable"
	"Lovers in Their Seventies"
The Town Crier	"Fairview"
	"The Messenger"

x

LETTING GO

POEMS
1983-2003

Contents

Before the Words Got Loud

Capture Those Moments So Rare

The Center of Things

Valley Words

What Really Matters

Shards of Color

LETTING GO

Before the Words
Got Loud

Photo of
Madge Liggett and Dean Lisle

Sepia Print: Nov. 2, 1919

They sit on the old wooden swing,
The sun on their faces.
They are nineteen and in love.
She leans against him
And looks as happy as
She said she once was.
Clasping her tightly,
Claiming her,
He is handsome and sober.

What did they know then of
Distances
That would cause him to
Loosen his clasp—
Her to move to the
Far end of the swing
Her smile fading?

We never saw those
November lovers,
Gone long before that
Rainy Saturday we spent looking
At the old picture album
And finding them there—
Two young strangers
In unfamiliar dress
And unfamiliar closeness.

We knew two gray persons
Meshed by
Forty years and
Four children,
Distanced by
The people they had become
Their hearts grown numb.

But we wished all our lives,
As children do,
To see those lovers in the print
Close on the swing.

And at last, 63 years later
In this sunless November ground
They are side by side again
With hardly any distance at all
Between them.

Clippings

All my life she would share with me
From ladies' magazines
Poems thick with sentiments
Of April loves, children
Growing, leaving home,
Cobwebs holding one
To duty, habit; craven kindness
Keeping prisoner one who would be free.
I filed them away
In some appreciation.
But patronizingly.
Too late I learned
It was not my literary airs
She meant to feed;
And others' slick words
Are the most I'd ever know
Of her reality.

Just Once

My daddy was tall and broad
With a Santa belly.
He was a truck driver and
Was not there most of the time
Which was all right with me
Because I was afraid of his
Deep voice, booming at my mother,
"Madge, can't you do a god-damn-thing
right?"
And even when he talked to me, it was,
"Bring me the damned hammer, child."
I thought he was mad
Most of the time,
For the only time I swore—
under my breath—
Was when my hair wouldn't go right
Or the crayon slipped outside the line.

But when I was seven and my story was
Printed in the Pittsburgh Sun-Telegraph,
He was the one who
Sat me on his fat lap and said
        just loud enough for me to hear—
"Look what you done," and smiling,
Read the whole article, out loud.
Then, "I think this calls for
An ice cream cone," the treat in 1937.

We must have gone to Grant
Confectionary,
But I remember only his soft lap,
His quiet words and smile.
It felt good to be His Girl,
Just once
On that dark January Ohio night,

Before the words got loud,
Before the fear set in,
Before he left again.

The Untouchable

When my hulking father
Was in outrageous pain
From what was soon diagnosed
As a ruptured aortic aneurysm,
My mother and I had to help him
Use the toilet, his arms draped
Heavy around our shoulders.
We could barely hold him up.
I was forty and it was the first time I had
Seen my father naked, and for my sake
I tried to act as if I wasn't really seeing
His penis, scrotum with only one testicle
I had heard about years before.

"Hold it, damn it," he growled in pain at my mother.
"It won't bite you."

In this scene where death
Was blowing icy
On all our backs,
Where pain brought him words
He'd never said before,
His anger seemed
An old anger.
In all those years,
Those forty-six years, had she
Ever done as he asked her that day?
This man she said she
Loved so much in their earlier years
She would take his clean shorts
From the clothesline and bury her face in them,
This man whose penis she could not touch.

Vulnerable

The autumn after the
Trauma of the upstairs bedroom
That I still cannot speak of,
I was too sick to go to school
For three months. Congested lungs
The doctor called it. I think
My nine-year-old self called it
Survival. I was sick all right:
Sick of hating/liking what my body felt
Which my Sunday school teachers—
Nor any other living persons—
Had ever spoken of.

The sickness got me out of that feared
Second floor bedroom
Down to the coal stove and mother
Whose cool hands felt soothing
On my hot head.

Finally, after months of her safe caresses,
The Campbell soups and oranges,
I had to go back to school.
The memory still smarts
Of that first day when I sat down
In a seat with something in it
And jumped up fast
And the whole class laughed.
That was too much for one
Who had become friends with
Being sick,
Had found safety in it,
Had forgotten for a while what it was like
Being vulnerable.

Words Retrieved

My metaphysical friend told me
That based on the belief that all words
ever spoken
Are still out there somewhere in time
And space,
Someone is trying to invent a machine
That will be able to sort through
And pick up
Napoleon's "The die is cast . . . ,"
Henry's "Give me liberty or . . . ,"
Jesus' "Blessed are the poor . . . ,"

I wish when he makes this machine
He would try real hard to find for me
The last whispered words of love
From my parents to each other,
Before all the years of estrangement.
And my mother's, to her third born,
"My darling child, I love you."
Words that I know were uttered
In some time and space,
Though I never heard them.

The News

Darling woman child
With wedding ring,
Husband, legal papers—
How happy I am for you
With your joyous news.

I want to
                wash your feet with sweet water
                kiss your face and hands
                caress your belly with
                        attar of roses oil
                and call each day to ask of
                        your burgeoning seed.

And maybe I can do
Enough for you to erase finally
From memory my mother's
Lowered head, my father's sighs,
Averted eyes, when I gave my news

About you—since I had
No wedding ring.
No husband. No legal
Papers. None of the things
That made such news happy

Except you.

Dean

Watercolor of Dean by
Donna Lisle Burton

Capture those Moments so Rare

Photo of Cassia and Tim
by Donna Lisle Burton

To My Sixteen-Year-Old Whom I Do Not Love Enough

On that small rocker now in our living room,
My mother used to sit on summer nights
In my bedroom, lit by the dim street light,
And watch in vain for my dad to come home
From playing cards. I did not understand
Her sighs, except they hurt me. That winter
I grew pale, and her hands were cool and light
On my hot face. But still not a kiss came.
When she saw you in my shamed womb
She did not stroke my head or sigh.
And even now, as time pulls her giddily
Through the years, with only her voice as before,
I want to crawl into that shrunken case
Where I knew I shared her with no one else.

Decision

When we moved to another state
In early August and my daughter was nine,
I was intent on making her
Independent. Right now.
I had a two-year-old who
Couldn't know why his world
Was different, overnight.
And I had to be smiling, solid for him.
I also had a new job to start
That looked bad from the beginning
And was.
Their father had to work a year
Of 4 to 12 while he was being
Broken in
And down.
And a nine-year-old just had
To help.

On the first day of school
I drove to the corner
And let her out to walk
The last half mile alone.
A nine-year-old could do that.

I drove away, watched
Her plod on,
Never looking back, never waving,
To a new school
Ten times the size
Of her last one.

I must believe that in another life
I will get the chance to make
Some important decisions
All over again.

Cassia

Watercolor of Cassia
by Donna Lisle Burton

His Daily Presence

When my son left home
For the last time
He was eager to
Get on his way.

The last week with nothing
But last-minute packing to do
He found himself pacing,
Biting his nails.

Isn't it time you got new
Stepping stones for the front lawn?
Those look shabby.
Off he went to the Stone Market.
Hot work, heavy work,
Something for him to do for two days.

What about my broken wind chimes
I said.
Oh OK he said
And that was two days' worth.

Those bushes look like hell Mom
Why do you let them get in such shape?
One more day.

Then it was time.
His face smiled and he waved as he left.
For me it was as hard as on the
First day of school at six.

But now when I feel
The loss of his daily presence
And wish I could still hear
His voice calling up from downstairs,

I gaze out the window
At the stepping stones, bushes.
And it's as if he's talking to me still
When the chimes sing their tunes in the wind.

That Heart

They watch the monitor
and have made gut-real
what they knew at brain level:
there is indeed a life in there.
The daughter and her husband's first,
and her first grandchild.
That minuscule heart
beating so fast
that when she tries to imitate it
she can't move her hand that quick.

For thirty years she's said
she would do it again,
before sonograms and given
the same circumstances.
But when he reached
into her and tore
it out and threw it away,
she didn't know
the heart
was beating,
fast as a jackhammer,
fast as a hummingbird's
wings, fast
as that heart.

Letting Go

Every piece of good
Advice says the same thing:
Let go. And I've been trying
To get my hands off everything dear,
Everyone important and give them
A push right out the airplane, over
The cliff, down
The waterfall, yahooing
As they go.

This relinquishing would not be so hard
If all along I'd had my fill.
Sucked that breast dry my mother claims
I readily gave up at three months.
Given myself fully to that child,
That friend, that love—
Then letting go would be
The completion of the act
Of holding on. It is much harder
When you've only touched,
Met with the eyes,
Stood in the same room,
Breathed the same air.

Only Eating

My second husband never understood
How his decision to cook for himself
(In view of the results of the angiogram)
Devastated me. He thought I would feel
Relieved of all the work—planning,
Shopping, cooking, serving—and glad to be.

He did not know that after years
Of arguing over whether the tomatoes
Should be sliced this thin or that;
Or the spigot turned on hard or slow;
Or the throw rug at the door placed here or there—
I could still place love on the table in a
Plate of fried chicken livers, cherry pie,
Potato pancakes—and for a little while
We could eat away our anger—together.

As his arteries unclogged, the last things
We shared melted away with the loosened
Plaque and for the few years we continued
To live together, we ate in silence,
He feeding himself and I, myself,
Each of us only eating,
Leaving the table starved.

Leaving

He sits typing
Long lists of do's and don't's
For while he is away—
    how to get rid of potato bugs,
    use fire extinguishers,
    apply calcium nitrate for blossom end rot.
I listen with a little ear
To admonitions regarding
Our sixteen-year-old son
And the car.

He's schooling me to do
Without him—
Beyond, that is, how I've
Already learned to do
Without him.

Except for our sustained mutual interest in
    growing cucumbers (the spineless ones),
    operating the outdoor sprinkler,
    and ridding the house of camel crickets,
We have been
Pulling apart
For so long
Death would be a cinch,
Divorce, a mere formality.

Backing Up To Truth

I heard a story about
A boy who went out
Pea-picking with his brother.
They had taken their new rifles with them
To try out on squirrels, jays.
And while climbing over a fence,
One brother's gun accidentally went off.

The boy went back to the field alone,
And picked peas for several hours.

Some time later he
Went to the sheriff and reported
What had happened.
Why didn't you come right away
The sheriff demanded
And tell us about your brother?

I don't know,
The boy said,
I had to pick peas.

The morning after our wedding night
I was sleeping deeply with my
Shiny wide gold wedding band on
When I was awakened suddenly
By hammer blows from the kitchen.
I've always wondered
Why my new husband
Had to make shelves
That
Morning.

Song on Hallowed Eve

Capture these moments
So few
When all is well
    all is well
Cries out its tune.

Soup pot is simmering
Wet steam
While all is dark
    all is dark
Outside my door.

Children are playing
Downstairs
I hear them laugh
  hear them laugh
Their secret fun.

I cut out patches
To quilt
Cut memories
    memories
Sew them for love.

Daddy is fixing
The door
His gift to us
    gift to us
To keep us warm.

Capture these moments
So rare.
Soon vanishing
    vanishing
Irrecoverable.

The Center of Things

Mark
Pencil drawing by
Donna Lisle Burton

The Messenger

I know the holy meaning of it all:
Christ child, star, Bethlehem, the inn too full.
I do not abjure all the liturgy
Of this season—its solemn cantatas,
Carols ripe with familiarity,
Or the eternally voiced messages
Of peace on earth.

But the promises they've made elude me.
Being of the twenty-first century,
I must have gone commercial—there it is:
Contaminated by the tinsel and the glare.
So, risking this disclosure, I admit
I find promises fulfilled, a little ecstasy!—
In a lighted tree.

To a Friend, Lately Divorced and Childless

Cats are good at this; slowly
They work their way in.
But animals allow choices
And euthanasia is
Acceptable.

There are more Causes than
Acronyms, each worthy
And demanding; but
Even your God knows you're
Dispensable.

Let something, then, claim you
That you cannot shake loose.
You love me rightly if sewn
In your pocket is a
Small juggernaut.

Thirteen-Inch Snowfall in Tuskegee, Alabama

In this land where winter never really comes,
Where fall is pale and indiscernible,
Where spring is just wisteria for a day,
It snowed and snowed one February day
As if to show it knew what winter was,
In this land where winter never really comes.

In this land where winter never really comes
And white is not considered beautiful,
Where collards are the order of the day,
Mid-western speech unintelligible,
Though I had failed, the forces found a way
To give us this brief compatible cause
In this land where winter never really comes.

Silences

The white halls echo my footsteps this still
morning. At the door a cross-stitch sampler .
advises me to have a good day. I move the switch

and am greeted by a tired and drooping
Christmas I came to dissemble so it won't
accost me in January. The paper-ring chain

has fallen over the standing box where the fair-haired
boy heads daily, content to move there, without
thought, desire or speech. The light-skinned child

with the long slim fingers often sits in the wheelchair
I push aside. When I put her on the floor, on all fours,
    she will stay
for a long time, wordless, staring at me. With one finger I
    roll the prone

stander back into the comer and think of the black-haired
    beauty
who stands in it daily at such an angle she could be a
    maiden
on the prow of a ship, soundlessly searching dark waters.

Again my laminated Monet has fallen behind the bolster
    chair
which weekdays holds a silent lamb in symmetrical
    position.
and allows her little spastic legs to relax a while. When my
    only talker

is struck, time and again, by her own lightening, curling
    her fingers,
stiffening her legs, sounds issuing from her that are not
    her,
I can only watch till it is done, both of us limp. I see the
    brief case

hanging askew from the desk of my thin scholar with the
     one
word vocabulary. "No" means anything, everything to
     him
and so it means nothing. Bulbs packed away, tree down,

Christmas is over here. I put out a few January snow
posters, cut snowflakes for the windows and I'm ready
now for the silence when the children return.

Margaret

Dear old friend,
we know what's going on here.
What medicine cannot understand
it names.
Your vision has always been
creative.
You do not stare to see;
you only glance
with that third eye.
As one seamstress to another
we know that with fabric in palm,
we move the thumb back and forth
over it, though not touching it,
to know it.

You tell me now you cannot see clearly
what you are looking at: the center is gone.
But I say to you
it always was.
You've just come into your own
my friend, and someone's given it
a name,
a pathology,
a thing to run from
I say at last you're free.
Relieved of facts,
you can now see as you've always seen,
looking at the center of things,
right at the heart
of them.

Mark the Epileptic

Even today, twenty years later,
I could move my finger in the air,
Trace a perfect profile of this child
With felt eyes, missing tooth, quiet smile,
All announcing normal six-year-old,
Until the lurching gait, drug-slurred speech,
Eyes that stare at things I couldn't see,
Made a pain in my throat with the thought
That this lovely boy, whom I once taught,
Would, even if he lived to be old,
One day be one of those shuffling ones
Seen in any day room where the funds
Are so restricted that the only
Recreation is always TV
Looked at by vacant eyes that stare at
Things you and I could never see.

Even today, I hope, mercifully,
One of those daily bolts of lightning
That robbed his humanness, frightening
His mother cold, took him at eight.

Please Do Not Go Beyond This Point
(Sign posted facing visitors' pews in Mepkin Abbey)

Please don't.
Stay clear of us.
Similarity between you and us stops here.
We have vowed obedience,
Chastity, poverty.
Hospitality to you.
But stay back there.

If you move closer
You might come to see
Why we chose this life,
Its austerity, routine.
Peace.
You may start to think
You want it too.

At this point is mystery
And you should stay here.
Beyond is
Holy water, altar.
Cross . . .
This is our world.
You stay back there.

Making Gethsemani Bearable

"[The architect's] plan was to remove the interior
Gothic shell of the century-old church and . . . expose
the stark structure beneath it. [He] wanted to strip
away the plaster and lath arches and fake vaulting to
reveal the simplicity of the church's bare brick
walls . . . which were [later] covered in white
paint . . . [He] advocated replacing the deeply hued
Munich windows with pale modern glass in patterns
of abstract geometric design . . . ."

The Abbey of Gesthsemani by Dianne Aprile

Everywhere only whites,
Blacks, browns.
Even the stained-glass windows,
Subdued shades of the
Same flat colors,
An occasional pale
Amber here and there.
No azure-clad heavy-lidded Madonnas.
No row upon row of
Brass candle holders
Gleaming bright flame reflections.

Seven times each day the monks
In their white, black, brown
Come one by one into the abbey,
Each genuflecting to the altar,
Then taking his seat in the Choir,
Slowly both sides—
Two rows facing each other—
Fill up with the neutral men.

But when they open their mouths
To sing and chant, nothing but
Rainbows pour out. The deep magenta
Of the basses booms forth.

The baritones, cobalt with fringe
Of bittersweet on the quick notes.
And the tenors—all peacock
With their trills,
Vermilion and gold.

I understand now the
Architect's plan.
The neutrality. Achromatic background.
All necessary
So the monks will not begin to
Dance to the music's passion
So the visitors can stay
In their seats without gripping the altar rail
So the walls and windows themselves will
Hold in place and not
Float away on iridescent clouds of sound
So the very abbey itself will
Cling to its foundation of
Ashen walls, pale monks.

Dilettante

What is the proper dress for middle age?
Always out of style, how could I know?
At nineteen, chastity belts were in vogue
And cigarettes—straight. Though I wore neither
Well, I complied. At twenty-nine when hands
Held white-gold wedding bands, I'd just thrown one
Away, and mine were filled with books instead
Which were not then in style in Steubenville.

I wore a blue-eyed blond in Tuskegee's dark halls.
At 35 I marched Montgomery's streets
With fat black arms around my neck—not bon ton.
When streakers and bras flew I was fully
Clothed, planting zinnias, celebrating
Twenty-five years of the same hair style.
At forty-one, when friends wore granny rings
With bright blue stones, I wore a son at my breast.

Now at fifty-one I sit in bed
Wearing flowered, thermal underwear,
Decorated with a calico cat
On my side and sporting a fat gray kitten
At my feet, while my husband is wearing
Mourning at the other end of the hall.
Her taste is all in her mouth, I hear them say.
It's always been that way. How could I change?

Connie

When I last saw my good friend
In the psychiatric ward I had to
Clutch the arms of my chair when she
Smiled at me. The top row of her
Once beautiful teeth were
Broken, snaggled, black.
See my teeth? she finally said.
Do you want to know what happened?
And told me a tale of a landlady
Who didn't like her, came
To her room one night
And beat her in the mouth.

It could have been that
Or any other scenario
When you're seventy,
Eat fear all day long,
Live on the streets,
Trust no one,
Forget you ever were a drum majorette,
Beauty queen, tango pro,
Exemplar teacher for twenty years,
And mother of two beautiful girls,
Grandmother of one whose
Beauty excelled your own.

Today she died
And I don't ever have to
See those teeth again
Those teeth that
Lied about my friend,
That denied her poise,
Her caliber
That broke my heart every time
She opened her mouth.

Valley Words

Photo of Steubenville, Ohio and the Ohio River
by Donna Lisle Burton

Shock Treatment

For over forty years
And at odd times
I have wondered what ever happened
To my roommate in the psychiatric ward.
She was tiny
And six months pregnant
But that made no difference.
There, everyone got
Shock treatment—the oldfashioned kind
Where you were awake and it took
Six people to hold you down as the electricity
Undulated through you
Finally putting you out.

I wondered then and I still do,
What did those obscenities
Do to that baby?
Did he one day die
With all those volts
Passing through his tiny body?

Or if he lives, does he still wonder,
At forty-four, about
The days he feels so
Violated—
        the dull head pain
        heart like a stone
        memory shorn—
Not knowing
Why?

The Mills

I turn a page in an art book
And see a painting of mills along
The Ohio River and my heart does
A flip-flop, like it will do
When after twenty years' absence
You turn a corner
On a once familiar street
In your hometown
And run into an old love.

Like that old love too, you remember
Only the shiny parts—the red glare
In the night sky made by the blast furnaces
Tapped, the mill whistles keeping time
In your life at 8 and 4 and 12
The glow on the river from all
The mill fireworks—
Pinks and golds and reds and whites—
And you forget how he made you cry,
Eyes smarting with soot and smoke—
How he made you sick, his callous bellowing,
Screeching, hammering,
Clanging night and day
And how he finally shortened your life
With his blackness falling over you everywhere
Making it hard to breathe, hard to see
The sun some days at noon
Or the stars and moon at night.

And like that old love,
Nothing compares, equals or even
Touches it. Not distance,
Time or new loves.
The river, the mills—
Nothing gets it out of you.

Birdie

Being a good teacher
And attuned to the benefit
Of the class as a whole,
And because I had the power
To choose who would and
Would not help make this
Class a manageable,
Presentable
Unit,

I decided Birdie would have to go.
For the good of the others, of course.

So after the Christmas party
(One has to be humane)

Birdie,

    who never looked at you
    but through you,
    spent most of her days
    turning over and over in her
    thin fingers a flat
    rectangular piece of
    yellow plastic, all the while
    scrutinizing it as if it were
    the Rosetta Stone,

    who tip-toed in and out of the
    linoleum squares on the floor
    as precisely as if programmed,

    who shrank away from any touch
    as if fearing
    irreversible contamination,

    who screamed shrilly in the middle

of the bean-planting scene of
"Jack and the Bean Stalk,"
who, without changing her
vacant eyes to anger
and while tip-toeing in the squares
to "Farmer in the Dell"
pushed Janie to the ground
and made her cry,

Birdie

who could only answer at lunch time
the question, "Does Birdie
want this orange?" with
"Does Birdie want this orange?"

Went.

By June the children
Were still asking,
"'When Birdie coming back?"

City Fall

One tree can make a fall
If that is all there is—
A flaming giant oak
Set near to me where I
Can see it every day
Til it turns brown and dies.

I do not need a vast
Countryside in view
To know that it is fall.
One flaming giant oak
Will do—if that is all
There is—one oak will do.

South Carolina Spring

I am content to let spring usher itself in.
Not totally ignoring the ubiquitous azaleas,
The wisteria looking about to drop
Its grapey bunches from my nameless gnarled tree,
Still, I cannot revel in a spring
Bought so easily as this.

For I can remember when the price was
Weeks of sooty snow, a foot off the curb
Into freezing slush, air so cold that breathing hurt,
Even standing still.
And when that green haze appeared
On bare trees and air still held a chill,
I knew it had been earned.

To You Old Lover, Wherever You Are

While I, too, am not one to
harken back to the
good old days
which, if they are ever to exist,
must surely be yet to come.
Nevertheless,
I would relinquish
the next few years
of this ordered existence
if I could be
working, one nearby
misty April morning
on an inert lump of clay,
hear you enter the studio,
and know without turning
that it was you,
my fingers suddenly making
sense with the clay,
my heart no longer keeping time,
since time had only to do
with when you were not here.

I mean to say,
it would be good
to see you.

Upon My Nine-Year-Old's Return From Summer Camp

No summer camps for me when I was nine.
Depression years meant two weeks' vacation
At Aunt Lou's in the country, out the pike.
And I was sick to come home. That eight miles
Ride by the Ohio River never seemed so long.
We arrived at that green time of summer
Evenings, that even then made flutterings
In my stomach. The whole world was green,
And everything a caricature of what
I had left. Flowers up past my knees;
Trees thick and dark inside; the long narrow
Sitting room, longer, darker than before.
And when my tall skinny kitten hunched
Her back and moved sideways back and stared
At me with round frightened eyes, I cried.

When the green was gone and the sumacs looked
Lacy black against the sky made pink
By the steel furnaces tapped, I sat with my
Mother—her profile slowly coming into
Focus—on the back porch swing whose squeaking
Seemed not so loud as when I first sat down.
Soon we climbed the long narrow staircase,
Paint peeling off the banister, up to
My stuffy room, where my bed, at least, was true.
And night, working the magic that she does,
Did it again. When I awoke to that
Summer morning—noisy cement trucks in
The alley, St. Paul's chimes ringing quarter til,
Friday bread smells drifting up from downstairs—
All dimensions were true again. I was home.

TIM

Watercolor of Tim
by Donna Lisle Burton

Doing It Over

Lately, in dreams of my first husband,
Whom I could not divorce fast enough,
He comes to me in a matter-of-fact way—
Not all smiling and loving as he used to be
Before I wore it out of him—but his
Let-me-see-how-I-can-fix-this-lamp-
And-make-it-work-again mode—
And I stand in awe, quiet, glad
He's back but also
Aware he is no longer mine,
Has come by out of kindness,
To help out.
              Forty years later, the script
Would read differently.
I would know I deserve that
Fine man, would now be
Spending all my later years with
His care and kindness
And not alone
While this other husband
Lives on the
Other side of town,
Still clueless as to
Why.

WHAT REALLY MATTERS

Watercolor of Alan
by Donna Lisle Burton

Falling in Love with a Boy from Across the Ohio River

I don't need to try to explain to him
that this dirty river runs through my veins
as well as between the states where we lived.
We both knew the river, the hills on
either side, the dirty mills in between.
Growing up five miles and a river apart
we might have gone to the same five-and-dime
in Steubenville at Fourth and Market Streets

on a Saturday to spend our little cache.
But what fifteen-year-old trombone player
would ever notice a ten-year-old girl
standing at the doll clothes counter? We must
have passed each other going opposite
directions on the bridge, he traveling
to my Ohio town to buy some school
clothes one August day and I going

for a trip to Aunt Lou's in the country,
just past his town in West Virginia.
Was he the tall thin dark-haired boy whose soft
brown eyes caught mine in that momentary passing?
Did he know even then that someday when
we were very old we would at last meet,
far from those hills, that river, that bridge and
fall in love, after we had each buried

our long-term mate and the larger part
of our lives was already spent? What caused
that fire between us when we finally
met? Was it the sparks from the molten iron
when the blast furnaces are tapped? Or
the river's blazing night reflections—the reds,
oranges and bronzes? Maybe it came
from the glint of the dime paid to the toll man

when we crossed the bridge. Or else from the shine
in our own eyes when we hear still
those valley words that only we know
the meanings of—smoke, dirt,
    hills,
          river,
              bridges,
                    mills.

Impetuosity

Do not hurry, my grown children say.
Be sure. Wait.
It's for your own good.

I imagine them whispering, *How
can she know what's best for her?*

Aren't their when-we-have-time
phone calls enough,
the mother's day across-the-miles cards,
two hours together at Christmas dinner,
and occasional visits from my only
grandson? What more could any
old woman want than that?

I'll tell you.

A hand on my leg that says I claim you.
A man who cannot hear from me too often.
One who also had forgotten the delight
of a well planted kiss, the luxury
of strong arms holding another to his chest,
the sweet surprise of an old body reawakening.
And more, even,
than that
an old woman could want.

Long-Time Companion

I sweep up the litter—each speck—
empty his box,
and brush each hair
from the rugs, chairs,

sofa and my yellow sweater
he lately purred
on, empty his
food bowls, put this

fluffy white mouse up he once played
With. Now no trace
of him is left
but in my heart.

Lovers in Their Seventies:
Answer to a Proposal Not Yet Offered

I think I would like to spend the rest of my life
sitting on our front porch, watching sunsets every evening
with your great arms around me, your broad chest
to put my face against and listen to your slow steady

heart. We talk the same language. We know tired,
the ache of bones, what forgetting is, that sudden
relief when the word, twenty minutes later, comes.
We are nice to each other and look way past supposed

shortcomings. We both know what really matters.
That you are comfortable and I am warm enough, that your
sweet tooth is satisfied and my feet rubbed toasty, that you
come
and that I wrap my arms and legs around you and hold you

when you don't. Old bear of a man, I don't need much
more than your sweetness and kindness to sustain my life.
And I hope what it is that you find good about me
nourishes yours—for whatever forever we have left.

Old Lady Teaching in Locker Room

The pool locker room was nearly empty,
only one white-haired woman there, white skin
doughy and puffy, towel partially falling
off her body, disclosing her mastectomy
scar, her lack of pubic and underarm
hair. I was just about to protect my
eyes from her when
                            she smiled and spoke about
how good the warm water felt and wasn't
this just the prettiest day ever and what
a good day to be alive. She smiled again
and she might as well have been fully dressed,
hat and gloves, even tea cup in her hand.
Then I knew what real self-confidence is:
knowing, knowing, you are not your body.

Prayers Offered for my Daughter, While Lying in Bed, Hearing Her Readying Herself for the Day

Be gentle with yourself,
your seventh graders, today.
Pack that with your lunch.
How fast your heels click
on your slick floors
as you move here, there,
in the yet dark morning.
Slow down, slow down,
for your heart beats as fast
as your heels click and hearts
wear out that way.

The door opens, closes—
you get the paper. Don't read it.
Don't let it accost your soul,
so soon out of sleep's reality.
Your darling boy dreams on
in his bed and I hear you
shush in to peek at him
before you leave. He does not
see you in the mornings but you are
there in his four-year-old clothes
you chose; daddy engineers dressing.

Big heavy angels, take note
of this working mother and be
with her all the day, lifting her
over the impossible spots
and holding her hand when it's only hard.
Don't send those fluttery gossamer
winged ones to her: she needs real help.
My hand cannot be there to cling to.
Heed this old mother's prayers;
send a martyr, a saint or at least
a very tough angel.

The Gift

David: Feb. 10, 1918-Jan.3, 1998

The plastic ivy in the nearby urn is bright aqua.
Another sports a trimmed Christmas tree,
orange bird atop. At your feet
is an unadorned young white oak.
The bronze of your plaque is scratched—
from a mower, I imagine.

I place pink pebbles on it from
the Holy Land
as one would for a Jew.
No matter that your marker says
Faithful Baha'i (I had that put on
knowing your desire), I'll always
think of you as a Jew.

In your suffering
You wished for so little.
But after eighteen days you said
I wish I could be in a room
With a peaceful scene outside and
A big window so I could see it and
The sunshine could come in.
Five days later you were here.

Do you know that I came today,
first visit in nearly two years?
It is unlike you to be
quiet so long.
I came today because
now I can—and because
it's your birthday
and because
I finally believe
you did the best you could:
my gift to us both.

68

Small white oak at your feet,
three giant ones on your left,
two magnolias across the road
A peaceful scene
with sun pouring down over all.

Time

When I no longer need Time,
I'll find it everywhere;
Ubiquitous as kudzu,
And just as hard to kill.

When I no longer want Time,
When white washes my hair
And all the things I've meant to do
Seem inconsequential

Then I'll be burdened with Time
The way the old ones are
Who worry how the years just flew—
And how today stands still.

Fairview

The view *is* fair from here and
as far as I can see.
Over the blue grey mountains in the distance and
when I step out onto my front porch
and see Georgia driving the tractor
in their scrumptious garden
(that we are often the beneficiaries of
and from which we have already been given
two bell peppers and one banana pepper)
these are fair views.

In how many towns can you see a corn field
a few lots down from the post office where
soon a sign will announce "Fresh Corn,"
and he means fresh for if he hasn't enough
ears picked when you stop by,
he'll excuse himself a moment, go pick
a few and bring them to you?
That's fresh corn my friend.

Our grocery offers most anything anyone
could need (even lox and pickled herring!)
and our pizza place has truly hand-made;
just like any tonky eastern city. And
sometimes at night where we live where there
are no street lights to mar the lovely darkness
of our gravel road, I think
this is the fairest of places, this Fairview,
and I am happy to be one of its newest citizens.

SHARDS OF COLOR

"Hostas"
photo by Donna Lisle Burton

Flowers from Old Seed

In my Master Gardener class
I learned I must not
keep the seeds from
this year's flowers
to plant next year.
Who knows what
maladies they contain,
what weaknesses they will
pass on, making the seed
sellers poorer.

Still I keep my
zinnia and marigold seeds
from year to year,
and true,
each year they are
less hybrid and spectacular,
all the while becoming
more commonly lovely
evoking days when I
walked through my
grandmother's garden and picked
marigolds, zinnias—just like these
sitting on my outside table,
picked for today's loveliness,
tomorrow's garden.

Cosmos

Anywhere.
They'll grow anywhere.
Scarlet, gold, yellow, golden-orange,
tangerine, pink, carmine, lavender,
white—each with a pretty
gold center.
All summer, into
　fall they bloom
Tall willowy pieces of
light, shards of colors,
they pander to the wind,
suck up to sun,
Faithful, faithful:
put them in sunlight
in ordinary soil
and they will greet you
every morning all
summer long then put you
to bed at night.
They dawdle until
　September
Wanting to stay as long
As the sun does.

Cosmos,
light of the Cosmos
some are called
bright lights.

Four O'Clocks

When the sun is causing other blooms
to droop or close up
the four o'clocks unfold into the sunset,
their little trumpet flowers, painting
the evening sweet and spicy.
Where are the people though
when the four o'clocks open?
I alone seem to see their splendor
while others are driving home from work
cell phones in hand
too busy to attend to necessities
let alone
four o'clocks.

Blush, cream, fuchsia, white,
and variegated they are.
When I step outside my kitchen door
on an early summer evening,
I smell them before I see them
Spicy sweet like carnations even
ten feet away.
Up close: heady.

They're called an annual
but they always come back
for they drop their large
peppercorn seeds each September
for a season of sleep, only to reappear
next June.

When I lived in the old house in the alley
all my growing up years
even though our front yard would
grow no grass, we had four o'clocks on each
side of the front steps.
Two little oases of brightness
in front of that dirty paint-chipped house.

Hostas

After the orange cheek-pink blossoms of the flowering
    quince,
after the hundred red blooms of the camellia growing
    tall as my old
rose of Sharon, even after the forsythia with its
    dripping
yellow droplets, the hostas start up like small green
    pencils.

Green and straight in the beginning, they curve
along the brick edging undulating near them
that soon they will hang over and obliterate when
they become fluted and variegated-bright

greens, cabbage-worm greens, nearly whites, each
a little bouquet of green, every year multiplying by
    two,
bringing me down on pained arthritic knees
to separate them, give them away, plant them
    elsewhere.

I brought these hostas from my parents' yard over
    twenty
years ago, on the plane, in a bag, soaked in water and
    a little
soil left on so they would not feel strange
so far from home and in a soil not rich and black

as they were used to but red with clay. I did not
    know
if they would survive the plane trip, the change
of climate, the red soil, but they are hardy dears
and they came right up first spring after.

I brought them down to this Egypt land, this place
I still reluctantly call home even after
thirty-six years. In Ohio they were in the shade of a
    huge red
 maple in the back yard by the garage which my father
    built

before he was too sick to do such things. He must
    have planted them
himself, as he was the gardener in our family.
    And I always
loved them in their cool blooming in the dark
back yard but something must have told me

*Take them now—or maybe never—*for in a few
years both parents had died and the house was sold
and then they were someone else's hostas, no longer
mine to enjoy, and dig up, and take with me.

They are the fifth sign of spring in my yard, before
all the dogwoods bloom, before each azalea
bush is shimmering in its showy glory, just
as the roses are developing their leaves

and aphids and the lambs' ears are still
mossy green, and look tender enough to eat.
When the snow-on-the-mountain,
the green and pink lenten roses,

the yellow and blue pansies are fully
blooming in front of my St. Francis,
with his bird in his hand, feeding it,
then the hostas appear.

In early summer before the sultry nights,
when the pansies are losing their pretty heads,
the hostas will send up a stalk of delicate and pale
purple flowers, signaling fullness of growth

and the impending ripeness of summer. But before
too long their flowers will fade and fall,
their leaves turn brown and melt and wilt
and they will go through an ugly dying

before they are entirely gone in October and I
can see no trace of them. But know
their tender bulbs are there, resting
after all the work of spring and summer

and surely as the sun rises in the east,
come March, even if I am not around
another year to greet them (I being far older
than twenty), they will arise, their little green fingers

shooting straight up out of the earth, through the
        pine straw,
through the dead leaves I need to get off the bed,
greeting me with their greenness like old reliable
friends, year after year after year.

Marigolds

Curious little seeds,
white and brown:
a piece of straw
dipped in chocolate.

Hardy, faithful, prolific
and bright. The French marigolds
are bronze and red.
Once I grew one called vanilla
snowball. Among other hues
of the red-orange family, they
come in titian, garnet, russet
and blond.

Last year I bought marigold plants
and they bloomed their heads
on and off all summer.
Fall doesn't hinder them either:
they don't know when to quit.

Hardy, camel like
(heat resistant is what the catalog says).
Piquant smell,
Put them around your peppers and the bugs
will run away. They're for eyes,
not noses;
but a nosegay of them
is nice.

Morning Glories

On our ramshackle paint peeling back porch
was a single breath of beauty. Each summer
my mother planted morning glories all
along the side, with the back porch swing
facing them As soon as they peeped
out of the soil, my father would put
little pegs in the ground by each azure
morning glory, run a string up to the roof
of the porch and before you knew it
the swing was shaded from the afternoon
sun by the morning glory vines.

Coaxed from their tight little folds
by the morning sun into large blue flowers,
they stayed out until the sun got
too high then folded back into
themselves to keep cool
and rest.

The vines though were lush and green
so even when the blossoms closed,
there was still that solace they offered
in their cool greenness,
a refuge of shade and beauty
on the dirty old back porch.

Petunias

I can find only annual petunias
in their purples, roses, pinks, whites,
variegated and occasional
yellows when I go looking for them.
But in the back yard of the old
dirty paint peeling house where
I first fell in love with flowers,
my mother had a bed of purple,
white and pink petunias that came back
every year. My dad had
cut up an old tire, put it on the ground,
and inside its circle flourished
these petunias. They gave
that yard where grass wouldn't even grow
something to feel dressed up about.

Early summer evenings you could sit
on the back porch swing,
shaded by the morning glory vines
and smell the spicy sweet tidbits.
Are they still blooming there
inside that old tire
even though the house
has been gone
for forty years?

Sunflowers

They will grow—and grow—and grow.
They are not finicky Sallies,
begging fecund soils,
rich foods. They need only
free sunshine, a little rain,
ordinary earth.

When my knees were no longer
good for seed planting positions,
I could still plant large
sunflower seeds.

                Get a broom handle,
pound a hole in the soft earth,
and standing, drop the seed in,
toe the dirt over the hole—
it's done.

Brick red, carrot, gold, variegated—
some are taller than I by several feet.
All brown seed centers
birds love to eat, clicking
their hulls to the ground.
Five inches across.
Ten inches across.
They will not fail you.
One is a bouquet.

www.ingramcontent.com/pod-product-compliance
Lightning Source LLC
LaVergne TN
LVHW021539080426
835509LV00019B/2739